# Tweeg and the Bounders

This story shows that a wish can be a wonderful thing
but trying to get something the wrong way usually backfires.

Story by:
Ken Forsse

Illustrated by:
David High
Russell Hicks
Valerie Edwards
Rennie Rau

**WORLDS OF WONDER™**

Grubby™  Newton Gimmick™  Princess Aruzia™  Leota™  Wooly What's-It™

Prince Arin™  Fobs™

Page 1

Tweeg had been trying for some time to make gold out of buttermilk.

Tweeg had been following a formula in an old book.

Tweeg always tries to get rich the easy way.

Tweeg doesn't realize
his greed is what makes
things go wrong.

The actual page about gold had been torn out of the book.